Agriculture Dictionary

Terminology of the Agriculture Industry

Edited by:
Cathy Caligiuri

Compiled by:
Dr. Michael A. Stachiw

Agriculture Dictionary: Terminology of the Agriculture Industry

Printed in the United States of America

Published by SM&DS through Createspace Independent Publishing Platform

ISBN-13: 978-1523715053

ISBN-10: 1523715057

Introduction

The first time a person encounters the language of the agriculture industry, they either become confused or they smile inwardly at the crystal clear meaning of the vocabulary. Like most specialized fields of science, the vocabulary and terminology has been developed to assist in the precise transfer of information between breeders, enthusiasts, farmers, veterinarians, and show officials. Incorrect usage and/or lack of understanding of agricultural terminology can cause miscommunication to easily occur.

The terms listed in this dictionary have been compiled from a variety of sources including 4-H documents from the Cooperative Extension, technical documents, trade journals, and those terms generally recognized and understood in agriculture. Some specific sources used in this document include the following:

Sources

- 1988. A Glossary of Farm Terms. United States Department of Agriculture, Washington, D.C.

- 1989. Understanding the Animal Model. National Association of Animal Breeders, Columbia, MO

- 2015. NAL Agricultural Thesaurus and Glossary, Washington, D.C.

- Campbell, J.R. and R.T. Marshall, 1975. The Science of Providing Milk for Man. McGraw-Hill Book Company, New York, NY. pp 739-769

- Krider, J.N. (editor), 1992, Animal Waste Management Handbook, United States Department of Agriculture, Soil Conservation Service, Washington, D.C.

- Stiles, K.A. and D.P. Dickson, 1985, Terminology - Fact Sheet A-6. National Cooperative Dairy Herd Improvement Program Handbook, National DHIA, Columbus, OH

Abdomen
The part of an insect lying behind the thorax.

Abortion
Premature expulsion of the fetus or unborn animal.

Abscess
A lumpy swelling or pocket of pus occurring in an animal's skin.

Acid
A chemical name given to many sour substances. Vinegar and lemon juice owe their sour taste to the acid in them.

Acid detergent fiber (ADF)
Fiber measurement extracted with acidic detergent in a technique employed to help appraise the quality of forages. Includes cellulose, lignin, ADIN, and acid-insoluble ash.

Acid detergent insoluble nitrogen
Non-digestible dietary protein or nitrogen.

Acid soil
Soil with a pH of less than 7.

Acre
Measurement of land area. 1 acre = 43,560 ft^2.

Acre-foot

The volume of water that would cover one acre of land (43,560 ft²) to a depth of one foot. 1 Acre-foot = 325,851 gallons of water. An acre-foot is the basic measure of agricultural water use.

Active ingredient

The component that kills, or otherwise controls, target pests in any pesticide product.

Ad libitum (ad lib)

At pleasure. Commonly used to express feed available on free-choice basis of the animal.

Adult

A person, animal, or plant grown to full size and strength.

Aerobic

Requiring oxygen. For example, many microorganisms require oxygen for the oxidation of food materials.

Aflatoxin

Aflatoxin is a naturally occurring mycotoxin produced by two types of mold: aspergillus flavus and aspergillus parasiticus.

Afterbirth

The placenta and allied membranes with which the fetus is connected with the mother. It is expelled from the uterus following parturition.

Aged

A horse which is seven years old or older.

Aging

Estimating a horse's age from its teeth.

Agronomy

The science of crop production and soil management.

AI daughter

Female offspring of an artificially inseminated female.

Aids

Whips, reins, spurs, and other items which help a rider convey instructions to the horse.

Air above the ground

Any movement performed with either the forelegs or the fore and hind legs off the ground.

Albino

Lack of pigment.

Alfalfa

Type of hay fed to horses.

Alkaline soil

Soil with a pH of more than 7.

Alopecia

Baldness; loss or deficiency of hair, natural or abnormal.

Also-ran

A horse that does not place in a race.

Amateur

A person who engages on an unpaid basis.

Amino acids

Building blocks of the protein molecule.

Ammonia

A colorless pungent gas, NH₃, composed of nitrogen and hydrogen; its compounds are used as fertilizers. A compound of nitrogen readily usable as a plant food. It is one of the products of decay.

Ammonium

An ion (NH_4^+) derived from ammonia (NH_3).

Anaerobic treatment lagoon

A structure to treat animal waste through predominantly anaerobic biological action using anaerobic or facultative organisms, in the absence of air, for the purpose of reducing organic matter in wastes.

Anaphylactic shock (Anaphylaxis)

A state of immediate hypersensitivity following sensitization to a foreign protein or drug.

Annual

A plant that bears seed during the first year of its existence and then dies.

Anorexia

Lack or loss of appetite. Eating disorder.

Antemortem

Before death.

Anterior presentation

Normal birth. The front feet and head of animal presented first.

Anthelmintic

A remedy for destruction or elimination of parasitic worms.

Anther
   The part of a stamen that bears the pollen.

Antibiotic
   A metabolic product of one microorganism or a chemical that, in low concentrations, is detrimental to activities of other microorganisms. Penicillin, tetracycline, and streptomycin are antibiotics. Not effective against viruses.

Antibody
   A protein (modified type of blood serum) developed or synthesized by lymphoid tissue of the body in response to an antigen. Each antigen elicits production of a specific antibody.

Antigen
   A high-molecular-weight substance (usually protein) which, when foreign to the bloodstream, stimulates the formation of a specific antibody.

Anvil
   Ferrier's tool used for shaping horseshoes.

Apprentice
   A youth who is being trained.

Arena
   Enclosed area.

Arid climate
   A dry climate with an annual precipitation less than 10 inches. Not suitable for crop production without irrigation.

Artificial insemination (AI)
Placement of fresh or frozen male semen into the female mechanically, without normal sexual contact.

Ascaris
Internal parasite, also known as roundworms.

As fed
Refers to feed as it is consumed by an animal, including moisture.

Aseptic
Preventing, or free from, contamination by microorganisms.

Atmospheric nitrogen
Nitrogen in the air. Great quantities of this valuable plant food are in the air; strangely, most plants cannot use it directly from the air, but must take it in other forms, as nitrates, etc. Legumes, however, are able to use atmospheric nitrogen.

Atrophy
A defect or failure of nutrition or physiologic function, manifested as a wasting away or reduction in the size of cell, tissue, organ, or body part.

Available plant food
Food in such condition that plants can use it.

Average daily gain (ADG)
The average amount of daily live-weight increase, as applied to farm animals.

Back
The entire top, or dorsal, portion of the animal extending from the neck to tail.

Back hoe
A hydraulically operated shovel mounted on the rear of a tractor to dig trenches or pits in soil.

Backstretch
Part of an oval racetrack furthest from the spectators.

Bacteremia
The presence of bacteria in the blood.

Bacteria
A name applied to many kinds of very small living beings, some beneficial, some harmful, some disease-producing. They average about one twenty-thousandth of an inch in length.

Bactericide
An agent or substance capable of destroying bacteria.

Bacterin
Vaccine. A suspension of killed or attenuated bacteria used to increase disease resistance.

Bacteriostatic
Describes a substance that prevents the growth of bacteria but does not kill them.

Bag
See udder.

Balanced ration
The daily food allowance of an animal, mixed to include suitable proportions of nutrients required for normal health, growth, production, and well-being. Such a ration avoids all waste of food.

Bale
A measurement of hay.

Baled hay
Forage that has been compressed into a bale (round or rectangular) to save space and aid in handling.

Balk
When a horse refuses to move.

Band
A group of horses.

Bareback
Riding a horse without a saddle or blanket on its back.

Barley
A grain often fed to horses.

Barren
Sterile, infertile, non-breeder, incapable of producing offspring. Open or not pregnant.

Barren period
The period of time during which a female does not conceive.

Barrow
A young castrated male hog.

Basal metabolic rate (BMR)
Turnover of energy in a fasting and resting organism using energy solely to maintain vital cellular activity, respiration, and circulation.

Basal metabolism (BM)
The chemical changes that occur in the cells of an animal in the fasting or resting state when it uses just enough energy to maintain vital cellular activity, respiration, and circulation as measured by the basal metabolic rate (BMR).

Basis
The difference between the current spot price or cash price of a commodity, and the price of the nearest future contract for the same or a related commodity.

Bedding
Material to make a horse box more comfortable.

Belly
Lower portion of the body containing the intestines. For the purpose of specifying a color area, it is the underbody, or ventral, portion of the animal from the forelegs to the crotch.

Biennial
A plant that produces seed during the second year of its existence and then dies.

Bioaccumulation
The absorption and concentration of toxic chemicals, heavy metals, and certain pesticides in plants and animals.

Biochemical oxygen demand (BOD)
A measure of the amount of oxygen consumed by natural, biological processes that break down organic matter, such as those that take place when manure or sawdust is put in water.

Biomass

The generic term for any living matter that can be converted into usable energy through biological or chemical processes.

Bit

The part of the bridle that fits in the horse's mouth.

Blaze

A white area on the head and nose running up between the eyes on animals with multi-colored fur.

Blemish

Any scar left by an injury.

Blight

A diseased condition in plants in which the whole or a part of a plant withers or dries up.

Blind quarter

A quarter of an udder that does not secrete milk or one that has an obstruction in the teat which prevents the removal of milk. A nonfunctional mammary gland.

Blistering (Firing)

The application of a hot iron to an animal's lower leg in an attempt to treat an unsoundness problem. The procedure is not well accepted because it is considered cruel and its effectiveness has not been proven.

Blood plasma

The liquid portion of blood in which the corpuscles of blood cells are suspended.

Bloodstock

Thoroughbred horses, especially those used for racing and breeding.

Blow up
   To buck. A term used to describe the behavior of a dressage or show horse which performs poorly.

Bluestone
   A chemical; copper sulphate. It is used to kill fungi.

Boil
   See abscess.

Bone meal
   Animal bones that are steamed under pressure and then ground. It contains 1.5 - 2.5% nitrogen, 12 – 15% phosphorus, and 20 – 34% calcium. It is used as a fertilizer and as a mineral supplement for feeding farm animals.

Bookie
   An individual who accepts bets.

Bordeaux mixture
   A fungicide invented in Bordeaux, France to destroy disease-producing fungi.

Botfly
   Parasitic fly.

Bovine somatotropin (BST)
   Also called bovine growth hormone; BST is a naturally occurring protein that has been genetically engineered as a synthetic compound that causes cows to increase the efficiency of milk production per unit of feed consumed.

Bovine spongiform encephalopathy (BSE)
   Commonly known as "mad cow disease," BSE is a slowly progressive, incurable disease affecting the central nervous system of cattle.

Bran

The seed coat of wheat and other cereal grains which is separated from flour and used as animal food.

Branding

Marking an animal for identification.

Break down

The back of the fetlock dropping to the ground, caused by a lacerated suspensory ligament or a fractured sesamoid bone.

Breaking

Training a horse to be ridden.

Breech presentation

Abnormal birth. The hind feet and rump presented first.

Breed

Animals having a common origin and characteristics that distinguish them from other groups within the same species.

Breeder

The owner of an animal at the time of breeding.

Breeding certificate

A written certificate by the owner of a male, showing the pedigree and the date of breeding to a particular female. Proof of ancestry of the young.

Breeding value (Genetic value)

The genetic ability or merit of an animal for a given trait, for example, speed. One-half of this genetic ability is transmitted to offspring.

Breeze

To win a race easily. A training sprint over a short distance.

Bridle

The headgear used to control the horse.

Broad-spectrum antibiotic
An antibiotic that is active against a large number of microbial species.

Broiler
A young chicken, usually 6 to 8 weeks old and 3 to 5 pounds, raised primarily for its meat.

Broken ear
A distinct break in the cartilage which prevents erect ear carriage.

Bronco
Any unbroken horse.

Buck
Male rabbit, deer or goat. When a horse jumps and arches its back.

Buck teeth
See wolf teeth.

Buckskin
A golden or tan colored horse.

Bud
An undeveloped branch. To insert a bud from the scion upon the stock to insure better fruit.

Bud variation
When one bud on a plant produces a branch differing in some ways from the rest of the branches. The shoot produced by bud variation is called a *sport*.

Buff
A golden orange color with a creamy cast.

Bushel
A dry volume measure of varying weight for grain, fruit, etc., equal to four pecks or eight gallons (2150.42 cubic inches).

13

Caked udders
A condition sometimes suffered by lactating females which leads to blocked and irritated udders.

Calyx
The outermost row of leaves in a flower.

Cambium
The growing layer lying between the wood and the bark of a tree.

Cannibalism
When a species eats others of its species.

Canon
The shank bone above the fetlock in the fore and hind legs of a horse.

Carbohydrate
An organic compound containing carbon, hydrogen and oxygen only; includes sugars, starches, and cellulose; necessary in the diet for energy.

Carbolic acid
A chemical often used to kill or prevent the growth of germs, bacteria, fungi.

Carbon
A chemical element. Charcoal is nearly pure carbon.

Carbon disulphide
A colorless, toxic, flammable chemical used to kill insects.

Carbonic acid gas
A gas consisting of carbon and oxygen. It is produced by breathing and whenever carbon is burned. It is the source of the carbon in plants.

Carcass weight
Weight of the animal after it has been processed.

Carriage
The way an animal carries itself; the style or characteristic pose of an animal.

Carrying capacity
The number of animals that a pasture can properly carry with feed for a certain period of time.

Cart
Two-wheeled vehicle.

Castration
The process of neutering a male animal.

Cavaletti
A series of small wooden jumps used in training to improve a horse's strength, stride, and balance.

Cavesson
A type of noseband used to keep the horse's mouth closed.

Cecotropes
The soft feces directly from the anus. *See night feces.*

Cecum
A pouch forming the beginning of the large intestine; fermentation process of digestion occurs here.

Cereal

The name given to grasses that are raised for the food contained in their seeds, such as corn, wheat, and rice.

Check-offs

The practice of deducting a portion of the payment to a farmer for his or her produce.

Cheek

The sides of the face beneath the eyes.

Chemical oxygen demand (COD)

An indirect measure of the biochemical load exerted on the oxygen of a body of water when organic wastes are introduced into the water. If wastes are readily biodegradable, COD and BOD are nearly the same.

Chest

The front portion of the body between the forelegs and neck.

Cholesterol

A white, fat-soluble substance found in animal fats and oils, in bile, blood, brain tissue, nervous tissue, the liver, kidneys, and adrenal glands. It is important in metabolism and is a precursor of certain hormones.

Chute

Straight part of a racetrack behind the barrier of the starting gate.

Classification

An appraisal program offered by a breed association to evaluate each animal's resemblance to the breed's ideal. A numerical score is assigned to each animal.

Clear round

A show-jumping or cross-country round which is completed without faults.

Close breeding
A form of inbreeding, such as mating brother to sister, father to daughter, and mother to son.

Cobalt
A hard, silvery-white, magnetic metal with Atomic Number 27. Important mineral for digestion.

Cobby
Stout and stocky. Short legged.

Cocoon
The case made by an insect to contain its larva or pupa.

Coggins
Equine infectious anemia.

Cold-blood
Any large, heavy horse whose ancestors originated in the cold regions of the world; particularly the draft breeds.

Colic
Digestive disorder.

Coliform bacteria
Bacteria from the intestinal tract of warm-blooded animals. Presence is considered indicative of fecal contamination.

Collection
Shortening a horse's pace by light contact from the rider's hands and steady pressure from the legs, which make the horse flex its neck, relax its jaw, and bring its hocks under.

Colostrum
First milk from the mother after giving birth. Rich in antibodies.

Colt
An ungelded male horse less than four years old.

Compact soil
Soil with closely packed particles.

Compaction
Closely packed feed in the stomach and intestines of an animal causing constipation and/or digestive disturbances.

Complete ration
A blend of all feedstuffs (forages and grains) in one feed. A complete ration fits well into mechanized feeding and the use of computers to formulate least-cost rations. Sometimes called total mixed ration or TMR.

Concentrate
A feed high in nitrogen-free extract (NFE) and total digestible nutrients (TDN) and low in crude fiber (less than 18 percent). Included are cereal grains, soybean oil meal, cottonseed meal, and byproducts of the milling industry such as corn gluten and wheat bran. A concentrate may be low or rich in protein.

Concentrated
When applied to food, the word means that it contains high feeding value in small bulk.

Conception
Fertilization or penetration of the ovum by a sperm cell.

Conception rate
Success rate of consumption. Calculated by dividing the number of conceptions by the number of inseminations.

Condition
Refers to the amount of flesh (body weight), quality of hair coat, and general health of animals. Also known as body condition.

Confidence range (CR)
Indicates the accuracy in the estimation of a male's genetic merit, therefore giving a probable range for future summaries.

Confinement
Livestock kept in corrals or housing for maximum year-round production. Facilities may be partial or complete, usually with a solid floor and enclosed or covered.

Conformation
The body form or physical traits of an animal; its shape and arrangement of parts.

Conjunctiva
The tissue covering the anterior portion of an eyeball.

Contact
The connection between the rider's hands and the horse's mouth made through the reins.

Contagious
A disease that can be spread or carried from one individual to another.

Cooperative
A form of business owned and controlled by the people who use its services.

Cooperative extension service (CES)
The state, university, and county educational outreach service of each state land-grant institution. This service extends the research results and educational programs of land-grant institutions to all the people in the state.

Coprophagy
The practice of eating droppings. *See cecotropes.*

Corn
A bruise in the area of the sole between the heel and the wall of the hoof.

Correlation
A mutual relationship or connection between 2 or more variables.

Course
A racecourse. In show-jumping and cross-country competition, a circuit including a series of obstacles which are jumped in a designated order, sometimes within a specified time limit.

Creamy
Very pale yellow or off-white color.

Creutzfeldt-Jakob Syndrome
A rare transmissible encephalopathy most prevalent between the ages of 50 and 70 years. Affected individuals may present sleep disturbances, personality changes, ataxia, aphasia, visual loss, weakness, muscle atrophy, myoclonus, progressive dementia, and death within 1 year of disease onset. Pathological features include prominent cerebellar and cerebral cortical spongiform degeneration and the presence of prions. Also referred to as mad cow disease when in cattle, and scrapie when in sheep.

Cribbing
When a horse chews on wood.

Crimped
Rolled with corrugated rollers. Crimped grain may be tempered or conditioned before, and may be cooled afterward.

Crohn's disease
An inflammation that may involve any part of the digestive tract from mouth to anus, mostly found in the ileum, the cecum, and the colon.

Cross
The result of breeding two different species together.

Cross pollination
The pollination of a flower by pollen brought from a flower on a different plant.

Crossbreeding
Mating animals of different breeds.

Croup
   The top of the hips.

Crude fiber (CF)
   That portion of feedstuffs composed of cellulose, hemicellulose, lignin, and other polysaccharides which serve as structural and protective parts of plants (high in forages and low in grains). Not soluble in acid or alkali detergents.

Crude protein (CP)
   Total protein in a feed. To calculate the protein percentage, a feed is first chemically analyzed for nitrogen content. Because proteins average about 16 percent nitrogen, the percentage of nitrogen in the analysis is multiplied by 6.25 to give the CP percentage.

Culling
   Removing from production/reproduction herd.

Culture
   The art of preparing ground for seed and raising crops by tillage.

Curb disease
   A swelling on the back part of the hind leg of a horse just behind the lowest part of the hock joint. Can cause lameness.

Curculio
   A kind of beetle or weevil.

Curing
   Preserving foods by using chemicals, smoke, sugar, or spices. May be used in combination with drying.

Cut
   To geld (castrate) a colt or stallion.

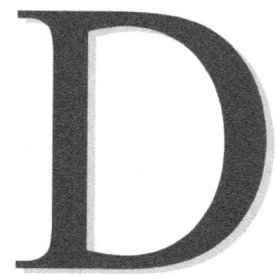

D

Dam

The mother of a foal.

Dark horse

A horse whose racing record is relatively unknown.

Dead heat

In racing, a tie for first, second, or third place.

Degraded intake protein (DIP)

That protein or nitrogen degraded in the rumen by microorganisms into microbial protein or freed as ammonia.

Dendrolene

A substance used for catching cankerworms.

Denitrification

The chemical or biological reduction of nitrate or nitrite to gaseous nitrogen, either as molecular nitrogen (N_2) or as an oxide of nitrogen (N_2O).

Density

The property or quality of a thick coat. Degree of compactness of a substance.

Deoxyribonucleic acid (DNA)

The chemical substance that is the principal nuclear material of cells. The structure of DNA determines the structure of ribonucleic acid which, in turn, determines the structure of proteins of the cell.

Dewlap
Fold of loose skin that hangs from the throat.

Dicoumarol
A chemical compound found in spoiled sweet clover and lespedeza hays. It is an anticoagulant and can cause internal hemorrhages when ingested by cattle.

Digest
To transform food into a form that can be absorbed by the body.

Digestibility
That percentage of food ingested which is absorbed into the body as opposed to that which is excreted as feces.

Digestible energy (DE)
The amount of energy actually digested by an animal (the amount consumed by the animal but not excreted in the feces). Digestible energy is broken down in the digestive tract, absorbed into the bloodstream, and carried throughout the body.

Digestible protein (DP)
The amount of protein in feed that is absorbed by the digestive tract; it may be computed using the formula:
Percent DP = Percent CP of feed x Digestion coefficient for protein in feed

Digestion
The act by which food is prepared by the juices of the body to be used by the blood.

Digestion coefficient
The digestion coefficient of feed ingredients (DCFI) may be calculated using the formula:

$$\text{DCFI} = \frac{Wt.\ of\ ingredient\ consumed - Wt.\ of\ undigested\ ingredient\ in\ feces\ \text{DCFI}}{Wt.\ of\ ingredient\ consumed} \times 100$$

Dismount
To get off of a horse purposefully.

Diuretic
A drug or agent used to increase flow of urine and feces.

Docking
Removing the tail for sanitation purposes.

Doe
Female rabbit or deer.

Dominant
Describes a gene that covers up the physical expression of its paired allele or recessive gene.

Dope
To drug an animal, either to improve or impair its performance in a competitive event.

Dormant
A word used to describe sleeping or resting bodies. Bodies not in a state of activity.

Draft horse
A horse used to pull heavy loads.

Drainage
The process by which an excess of water is removed from the land by ditches, terraces, or tiles.

Dressage
Classical form of horse training.

Dressing
See processing.

Dry matter (DM)
The moisture-free content of feeds.

Dyspnea
Difficult or labored respiration.

Dystocia
Abnormal or difficult labor (parturition), causing difficulty in delivering the fetus and placenta.

Earthen storage basin

An earthen pond or basin for storing animal waste. Differs from an anaerobic treatment lagoon in that wastes are not stored for an extended period and microbial breakdown or treatment does not occur.

Eclipse Award

An award for outstanding achievement in the Thoroughbred business, equivalent to the motion picture industry's Academy Award.

Edema

The presence of abnormally large amounts of fluid in the intercellular tissue spaces of the body, as in swelling of mammary glands commonly accompanying parturition in many farm animals.

Efficacy

The ability to produce a desired or intended result. Effectiveness.

Effluent

The liquid outflow or discharge of a waste treatment process.

Electrolytes

A substance which separates into two or more ions when it is dissolved in water.

Electrophoresis

An electrochemical process in which macromolecules or colloidal particles with a net electric charge migrate in a solution under the influence of an electric current.

Element
  A substance that cannot be divided into simpler substances.

Emaciation
  A wasted condition of the body; great losses of body weight or condition.

Embolism
  An obstruction in an artery. Typically a blood clot or an air bubble.

Embryo
  The early stages of fetal development inside the female.

Embryo transfer
  Modern technology whereby multiple fertilized eggs (ova) are flushed from the donor's uterus, and are transferred to a recipient animal that serves as a surrogate mother. The fertilized ova may be frozen and stored indefinitely before they are thawed and transferred to recipients.

Ensilage
  A green chop (forage) preserved by fermentation in a silo, pit, or stack, usually in chopped form.

Enteritis
  Intestinal inflammation caused by bacteria, poison, or moldy feed which contains fungi.

Epidemic
  The rapid spreading of a disease so that many animals or people have it concurrently.

Epizootic
  Designating a widely diffused disease of animals spreading rapidly and affecting many individuals of a kind concurrently in any region, thus corresponding to an epidemic in man.

Equestrian
  Pertaining to horsemen or horsemanship. A rider on horseback.

Equine
   Pertaining to horses.

Equine sports medicine
   The science of equine athletic conditioning and related factors. Still in its infancy, the science began by adapting human athletic conditioning principles to performance horses. It utilizes scientific technology in an attempt to improve the athletic performance of horses. Equine sports medicine includes the study of all areas which can impact performance, such as body function mechanisms (nutrition/digestion, cardiovascular and respiratory functions, bone density, blood composition, bone/muscle function, etc.), gait and motion analysis, and training/conditioning techniques. At this time, the science primarily impacts racing, but is expected to expand to other performance activities in the near future.

Ergosterol
   A plant sterol which, when activated by ultraviolet rays, becomes vitamin D2, also called provitamin D2 and ergosterin.

Eructation
   The act of belching or casting up gas from the stomach.

Estrous cycle
   Recurring 14 to 16 day cycle when a female will conceive.

Estrus (oestrus, estrous)
   The recurrent, restricted sexual receptivity (heat) in female mammals, commonly marked by intense sexual urge. Estrous pertains to the entire cycle of reproductive changes in the nonpregnant female animal.

Ether extract (EE)
   Fatty substances or lipids of foods and feeds that are soluble in ether.

Evaporate
   To pass off in vapor. To change from a solid or liquid state into vapor, usually by heat.

Event horse
   A horse which competes in the three-day event.

Exacta
   A type of bet in which the wagerer must choose the first and second place winners and the order in which they finish in order to win.

Exhaustion
   The state in which strength, power, and force has been lost. When applied to land, the word means that land has lost its power to produce well.

Exocrine (eccrine)
   Secreting outwardly, into, or through a duct.

Extra label use drug (ELUD)
   An antibiotic or other chemical used on the advice of a veterinarian in a dosage, route of administration for a disease, or in some other manner not included on the approved printed package label.

Eye circle
   Even marking of color around both eyes.

Eye color
   The color of the iris.

False heat
The display of estrus by a female animal when she is pregnant.

Farrier
An individual who makes horseshoes and puts shoes on horses.

Fats
Organic compounds found in vegetable and animal oils that are necessary in the diet.

Fault
In jumping, a scoring unit which penalizes a competitor for knockdowns, refusals, falls, touches (touching the obstacle) or other mistakes. Imperfections. Conditions or characteristics that are unacceptable and will result in lower show placing but not disqualification.

Feature race
The main race of a race event.

Fecal coliform bacteria
See coliform bacteria.

Federation of cooperatives
An organization of cooperatives that provides for joint activities but allows each cooperative to manage its own affairs.

Federation Equestre International (F.E.I.)
Also known as the International Equestrian Federation, it is the world's governing body of international equestrian sport. Founded in 1921, the F.E.I. is headquartered in Brussels. It makes the rules and regulations for international equestrian competitive events, including the Olympic Games, the Pan American Games, and the World Championships. All national equestrian federations are required to comply with the F.E.I.'s regulations in international competition.

Feed conversion
The amount of feed used compared to the amount of weight gained (ratio of feed to weight gain).

Fence
Any obstacle which must be jumped in hunting, show- jumping, cross-country, or steeplechase competition.

Fermentation
A chemical change produced by bacteria and yeast. A common example of fermentation is the change of cider into vinegar.

Fertility
The state of being fruitful. Land is said to be fertile when it produces well.

Fertilization
The act which follows pollination and enables a flower to produce seed.

Fetlock
The long-haired cushion on the back side of a horse's leg just above the hoof.

Fetus
The developing young, still within the female's uterus.

Fiber
   The cellulose portion of roughages (forages) that is low in TDN and hard to digest by monogastric animals.

Field performance trial
   Tests on the effectiveness and efficiency of feeds under real-life conditions, outside the research center.

Filly
   A female horse less than four years old.

Filter
   To purify a liquid, such as water, by causing it to pass through a substance such as paper, cloth, or screens.

Fingerlings
   Young immature fish less than one year old, 2-25 cm long. Often used for stocking, line feeds, and bait.

Flabby
   The condition when the flesh or fur hangs loosely. Not trim and shapely.

Flank
   The sides of an animal between the ribs and hips and above the belly.

Floating
   The process of filing down sharp teeth.

Flushing
   Putting females on an increasing plane of nutrition prior to breeding to increase ovulation and fertility.

Fly back
   Prompt and even flowing back of the fur that has been stroked from the tail towards the head.

Foal
A male or female horse less than one year old.

Fodder
Coarse food for cattle or horses, such as corn stalks or straw.

Forehand
The part of the horse which is in front of the rider; head, neck, shoulders, withers, and forelegs.

Forehead
The front part of the head between the eyes and the base of the ears.

Formalin
A forty percent solution of a chemical known as formaldehyde. Formalin is used to kill fungi and bacteria.

Formula
A recipe for the making of a compound; for example, fertilizer or spraying compounds.

Foster out
Moving a newborn from a litter too large for the mother to feed to a mother with fewer babies.

Founder
Severe laminitis.

Free-choice
A feeding system that allows animals to eat at will. *See self-feeder.*

Freeze drying
The evaporation of water from a frozen product with the aid of high vacuum. Also called lyophilization.

Frog
The elastic, horny center of the sole of a horse's hoof.

Fryer

Young meat. Rabbit less than five pounds.

Fungicide

A substance used to kill or prevent the growth of fungi; for example, Bordeaux Mixture or copper sulphate.

Fungous

Belonging to or caused by fungus.

Fungus (plural fungi)

A low kind of plant life lacking in green color. Molds and toadstools are examples.

Furlong

1/8 of a mile or 220 yards.

Gait
    Any forward movement of an animal, such as walking or running.

Gall
    A sore on the skin caused by chafing. Especially common on horses under the saddle or girth.

Gallop
    Fastest a horse can run.

Gaseous products of digestion (GPD)
    The combustible gases produced in the digestive tract during fermentation of the ration. Methane constitutes the major proportion of the combustible gases produced by ruminants. Non-ruminants also produce methane. Trace amounts of hydrogen, carbon monoxide, acetone, ethane, and hydrogen sulfide are also produced.

Gastroenteritis
    Chemical, bacterial, or viral inflammation of the mucosa of the stomach and intestines.

Geld
    To castrate a male horse.

Gelding
    A male horse that has been castrated.

Genetic merit
The genetic value of the animal used in a breeding program. *See breeding value.*

Genetic trend
Genetic change per year for a trait in the population.

Genotype
The actual genetic constitution (makeup) of an individual as determined by its germ plasm. *See dominant.*

Germ
A very small organism or living thing. Particularly one that causes great effects such as disease and fermentation.

Germinate
To sprout. A seed germinates when it begins to grow.

Gestation pregnancy
The time from conception to birth.

Get
The offspring of a sire.

Gilt
A young female hog.

Girdle
To make a cut or groove around a limb or tree.

Girth
The circumference of a horse measured around the deepest part of the body behind the withers. A strap around the horse's girth which holds the saddle in place.

Giving milk
Lactating. The act of yielding milk by a mammal.

Globule
 A small particle of matter shaped like a globe.

Glossy
 The reflection of luster or brightness from naturally healthy fur.

Glucose
 A kind of sugar found in plants. For example, the sugar from grapes and honey is glucose. That from the sugar cane is sucrose.

Gluten
 A form of protein found in grains.

Going
 The condition of a race track or other ground over which an animal travels, such as "good going" or "muddy going."

Goitrogenic
 Producing or tending to produce goiter (enlargement of the thyroid gland).

Gossypol
 A toxic yellow pigment found in cottonseed. Heat and pressure bind it with protein and thereby render it safe for animal consumption.

Graft
 To place a living branch or stem on another living stem so that it may grow there. This ensures the growth of the desired kind of plant.

Granule
 A small grain.

Graze
 To consume vegetation while standing, as by livestock or wild animals.

Green

A horse which is broken but not yet trained. A trotter or pacer which has not been raced against the clock.

Green chop (fresh forage)

Forages harvested (cut and chopped) in the field and hauled to livestock. This minimizes the loss of moisture, color, nutrients, and waste. Also called zero grazing or soilage.

Groom

An individual who is responsible for looking after a horse. To clean the coat, mane, tail, and feet of an animal.

Gross energy (GE)

The amount of heat, measured in calories, released when a substance is completely oxidized in a bomb calorimeter. The total amount of energy provided in the animal's feed.

Growth

Describes an animal that is large and well-developed for its age.

Hack
> A riding horse for hire. A pleasure ride.

Hackamore
> A bridle that controls the horse by pressure on its nose.

Half-sibling
> A half-brother or half-sister. Siblings who share the same mother or father, but not both.

Hand
> Measurement used to determine the height of a horse. A hand equals four inches, the average width of a man's hand. A horse's height is measured from the highest part of the withers to the ground. The abbreviation for height is h.h. (hands high). Fractions of a hand are expressed in inches. For example, a horse 15.2 hands high is 15 hands, 2 inches tall.

Hardware disease
> Commonly, an inflammation of the body cavity by an animal eating metal objects and perforation of the digestive tract.

Haunches
> The hips and buttocks of an animal.

Hay
> Dried forage (e.g., grasses, alfalfa, clovers) used for feeding farm animals.

Haylage
Low-moisture silage (35 to 55 percent moisture). Grass and legume crops are cut and wilted in the field to a lower moisture level than normal for grass silage, but the crop is not sufficiently dry for baling. It is commonly stored in a sealed or airtight storage system.

Hayloft
Second story of a building where hay is stored.

Heart girth
The circumference of the body just behind the shoulders of an animal. It is used to estimate body weight.

Heat
See estrus.

Heat increment (HI)
The increase in heat produced following consumption of food. It consists of calories released in fermentation and nutrient metabolism. When environmental temperature is below critical temperature, this heat may be used to keep the body warm; therefore, it is not wasted. Also called work of digestion.

Heat period
That period of time when a female will accept a male in the act of mating. Also called in heat or estrus. *See estrous cycle.*

Hectare
A metric unit of land measurement equal to 2.47 acres.

Herd
A group of animals collectively considered as a unit.

Heredity
The passing of physical or mental characteristics genetically from one generation to another.

Heritability

The proportion (fraction) of difference among animals for a trait due to genetic difference rather than environmental factors. The fraction of variation in a trait that is genetically transmissible from parent to offspring.

Hibernation

To pass the winter in a torpid or inactive state in close quarters.

High-moisture silage

Silage usually containing 70 percent or more moisture.

Hindquarters

See quarters.

Hip

The thigh joint and large muscular first joint of the hind leg.

Hives

An allergic reaction characterized by bumps on the skin.

Hock

The joint in the hind leg of quadrupeds between the leg and the shank. It corresponds to the ankle in humans.

Homestretch

Part of an oval track closest to the spectators.

Host

The object upon which a parasite is preying.

Hot-blood

Any light, fast horse whose ancestors originated in the hot, dry areas of the world; particularly the Arabian breed.

Hump back

The condition of having a hump or protrusion on the back, marring an otherwise gracefully arched outline.

Humus
The portion of the soil caused by the decay of organic matter.

Hybrid
The result of breeding two different kinds of plants or animals together.

Hydrogen
A chemical element. It is present in water and in all living things.

Hypoglycemia
Below normal blood glucose level.

Immunity
The power an animal has to resist and/or overcome an infection to which most of its species is susceptible. Active immunity is attributable to the presence of antibodies formed by an animal in response to anti-genetic stimulus. Passive immunity is produced by the administration of preformed antibodies.

Impaction
Constipation. *See compaction.*

In foal
In gestation.

In vitro
Within an artificial environment, as within a test tube.

In vivo
Within the living body.

Inbreeding
The mating of related animals, such as brother and sister or son and mother.

Individual
A single person, plant, animal, or thing of any kind.

Infertility
The inability to become pregnant or to produce offspring.

Inherited
Traits or characteristics passed on from a parent to offspring.

Inoculate
To give a disease by inserting the germ that causes it into a healthy being.

Insectivorous
Anything that eats insects.

Intake protein (IP)
Total protein or nitrogen consumed without regard to quality.

Intermediate
A show class term referring to rabbits that are at least six months old and no older than eight months and that fulfill the weight requirements of the breed.

International Unit (IU)
A unit of activity or potency for vitamins, hormones, or other substances, defined individually for each substance in terms of activity of a standard quality or preparation. Unit measurement is defined by the ICUF. Also called USP unit.

Intestinal flora
The microorganisms present in the intestine; some are required for digestion.

Iris
The circle of color in an eye surrounding the pupil.

Irrigation
Application of water to soil for the purpose of plant production.

Islets of Langerhans
Groups of pancreatic cells that secrete insulin and glucagon.

Jack
   Non-castrated male donkey.

Jaundice
   Characterized by a yellowing of the skin and whites of the eyes. Usually caused by liver disease, obstruction of the bile duct, or excessive breakdown of red blood cells.

Jenny
   Female donkey.

Jockey
   Professional rider of racehorses.

Jodhpurs
   English riding pants.

Jump-off
   In show jumping, a round held to decide the winner among those competitors who tied for first place in the previous round.

Jumper
   Any horse trained to compete over jumps.

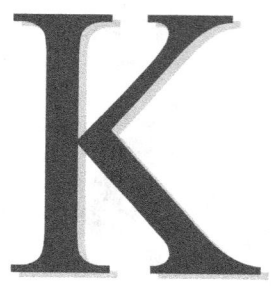

Kainit
Salts of potassium used in making fertilizers.

Kernel
A single seed or grain, such as a kernel of corn.

Ketone bodies
Any of three related compounds (acetone, acetoacetic acid, and beta-hydroxybutyric acid) produced during the metabolism of fats.

Ketosis
A metabolic disease characterized by an elevated concentration of ketone bodies in body tissues and fluids. Associated with abnormal metabolism and diabetes mellitus.

Kilocalorie (kcal)
Equivalent to 1000 calories.

Kindling
The birth process in rabbits.

Kit
Baby rabbit.

Knee
The second joint on the leg. In animals, more properly called the hock. The second joint of the foreleg is called the elbow.

Lachrymation
The act of tearing. Secreting and conveying tears.

Lactate
To secrete or produce milk.

Lactation
Production of milk.

Lagoon
See anaerobic treatment lagoon.

Lame
Moving stiffly or with a limp.

Laminitis
Hoof disease.

Larva (plural larvæ)
The young or immature form of an insect.

Larval
Belonging to larva.

Layer
To propagate plants by a method similar to cutting. The difference being that the young plant takes root before being separated from the parent plant.

Leaching

The process of removing soluble materials by the passage of water through soil.

Legume

Clovers, alfalfa, and similar crops that can absorb nitrogen directly from the atmosphere through action of bacteria that live in their roots and use it as a nutrient for growth.

Length

The length of a horse's head and body, used to measure the distance by which a horse wins a race.

Libido

Sexual desire or instinct.

Lichen

A flowerless plant that grows on stones, trees, boards, etc.

Ligament

Fibrous tissue that connects bones in a joint.

Lignin

A compound which, with cellulose, forms the cell walls of plants. It is practically indigestible.

Line breeding

A breeding program involving the mating of animals that are both descended from the same animal and are related several generations back. For example: mating first cousins, uncle to niece, or aunt to nephew.

Lipid

Any one of a group of organic substances that are insoluble in water though soluble in alcohol, ether, chloroform, and other fat solvents, and have a greasy feel. They are rich sources of dietary energy.

Liquid-solid separation
The process of passing a liquid-solid suspension, such as animal manure, over a screen or similar device to partially remove solids prior to storage or application.

Litter
Young animals born at the same time.

Loam
An earthy mixture of clay and sand with organic matter.

Lockjaw
Bacterial infection caused by Clostridium Tetani.

Long feed
Coarse or unchopped feed such as hay, as contrasted with short or chopped feed.

Loose coat
The condition of fur lacking density in the undercoat, coupled usually with fine guard hairs and resulting in lack of texture. Does not indicate a slipping coat.

Loose housing
Facilities which allow livestock access to a large, open bedded area for resting. Also known as free housing. Loose housing provides at least 200 square feet per animal for feeding and resting while free stall housing uses only 90 square feet per animal.

Low-moisture silage
Silage that contains 35 to 55 percent moisture. *See haylage.*

Lucerne
A legume of high feeding value for ruminants.

Lunge
A long line, usually fifteen to twenty feet long, used in training. One end of the lunge is attached to one side of the bridle; the trainer holds the other end in his hands as the horse circles him.

Magnesia

An earthy white substance somewhat similar to lime.

Magnify

To make larger in fact or appearance. To enlarge the appearance of something so that the parts may be seen more easily.

Maiden

A horse of either sex which has not won a race.

Maiden mare

A mare which has not had a foal.

Malocclusion

An inherited defect where the upper and lower jaws do not let the teeth meet, resulting in long, uneven teeth extending out of the mouth.

Mandolin

The shape of a rabbit's body. It resembles the shape of a pear and the musical instrument from which it gets its name.

Mane

Long hair growing from a horse's neck.

Manure

The fecal and urinary excretions of livestock.

Mare

A female horse more than four years old.

Marked
   A rabbit's fur, usually white, which is broken up by an orderly placement of another color. Also refers to rabbits that carry the pattern of the Tan variety.

Martingale
   An aid used to help keep a horse's head in the correct position. It usually includes a strap running between the forelegs which connects the girth and the front of the bridle.

Mastectomy
   Removal of the mammary glands.

Mastitis
   An inflammation of the mammary gland, usually caused by bacteria.

Match
   A race between two horses, on terms agreed by their owners.

Meconium
   Dark brown or black fecal matter passed by a foal shortly after birth.

Mee
   The place where hunters, horses, hounds, and followers gather before a hunt.

Megacalorie (Mcal)
   Equivalent to 1000 kcal or 1,000,000 cal. A megacalorie is equivalent to a therm.

Membrane
   A thin layer or fold of animal or vegetable matter.

Metabolic weight
   The weight of an animal raised to three- quarter power (W0.75).

Metabolizable energy (ME)
Food-intake gross energy minus fecal energy, energy in the gaseous products of digestion (mostly methane), and urinary energy.

Metabolize
To undergo change in a complex physical or chemical manner; necessary for the maintenance of life.

Metritis
An inflammation of the uterus.

Mildew
A growth of fungi on diseased or decaying objects.

Mineral
A substance neither animal nor vegetable, but inorganic, such as iron and other elements; many minerals are necessary in the diet of rabbits.

Miss
See pass.

Mold
See mildew.

Molt
The process of shedding or changing the fur or feathers twice each year. The baby or nest fur is molted at two months.

Monogastric
Having only one stomach or stomach compartment, as do humans, dogs, and swine.

Mortalities
Deaths.

Mount
To climb onto.

Muck out
   To remove manure and soiled bedding from an animal's stall.

Mudder
   A horse which races well on a muddy track.

Mulch
   A covering of straw, leaves, or like substances over the roots of plants to protect them from heat and drought, and to preserve moisture.

Mule
   Hybrid of a horse and a donkey.

Mummified fetus
   A shriveled fetus that has remained in the uterus instead of being aborted or expelled. Fluids from the fetus have been partially reabsorbed by the mother.

Mustang
   Any wild horse. Particularly the wild horse of the western plains of the U.S., which is descended from Spanish horses.

Muzzle
   The projecting portion of the head surrounding the mouth, nose, and lower jaw.

NAAB stud code
An identification number composed of a one or two digit prefix indicating the AI stud and a letter indicating the breed of the male specie. The remaining numbers identify the male within a stud.

National Association of Animal Breeders (NAAB)
The national organization made up of representatives from the artificial insemination (AI) industry.

National Research Council (NRC)
A division of the National Academy of Sciences established in 1916 to promote the effective use of scientific and technical resources. This private, nonprofit organization of scientists publishes bulletins periodically giving nutrient requirements of domestic animals.

Natural service
In farm animals, it means to allow natural mating, as opposed to artificial insemination.

Near Side
The horse's left-hand side, from which it is usually mounted.

Neck
The part of the animal connecting the head and body.

Nectar
A sweetish substance in blossoms of flowers from which bees make honey.

Neonatal
   Pertaining to a newborn animal.

Net energy (NE)
   The difference between metabolizable energy and heat increment.
   It includes the amount of energy used either for maintenance only
   or for maintenance plus production.

Neutral detergent fiber (NDF)
   A measurement of fiber after digesting in a non-acidic, non-
   alkaline detergent as an aid in determining quality of forages.
   Contains the fibers in ADF, plus hemicellulose.

Nick
   Mating that produces offspring superior to either parent.

Night feces
   Soft feces produced at night, higher in vitamins with a gel like
   consistency.

Nitrate
   A final decomposition product of organic nitrogen compounds. A
   nitrogen-oxygen ion (NO_3-) available as a plant nutrient and
   soluble in water.

Nitrification
   The biochemical transformation by oxidation of ammonium (NH_4)
   to nitrite (NO_2) or to nitrate (NO_3).

Nitrogen
   Colorless, odorless, unreactive gas that forms 78% of the earth's
   atmosphere.

Nitrogen-free extract (NFE)
   Consisting of carbohydrates, sugars, starches, and a major portion
   of materials classed as hemicellulose in feeds. When crude protein,
   fat, water, ash, and fiber are added and the sum is subtracted from
   100, the difference is NFE.

Nodule

A little knot or bump.

Non-point source

Entry of pollution into a water body in a diffuse manner so there is no definite point of entry.

Noseband

The part of a bridle which lies across the horse's nose, above the bit.

Nutrient

Any substance which nourishes or promotes growth.

Oats
> A cereal grain harvested for its edible seed. Commonly fed to horses.

Odds
> The betting quotation on a horse in a race.

Oestrus
> *See estrus.*

Off colored
> Applied to several hairs or patches of fur foreign to the standard color of the animal.

Off feed
> Having ceased eating; without a healthy and normal appetite.

Off side
> A horse's right-hand side.

On its toes
> Refers to a horse which is eager to keep moving.

Open
> A term commonly used for non-pregnant farm mammals.

Open coat
> *See loose coat.*

Organic matter
Substances made through the growth of plants or animals.

Organic nitrogen
Nitrogen bound in organic compounds, such as protein or amino acids. Requires microbial decomposition prior to nitrification as a plant nutrient.

Out of
Mothered by inter-animal breeding.

Outbreeding
A breeding program involving the mating of unrelated animals of the same breed.

Outcross
Mating one individual to another in the same breed who is not closely related to it.

Outlaw
Rouge horse that resists human handling.

Ovariectomy
The surgical removal of an ovary.

Ovary
The particular part of the pistil that bears the immature seed.

Over-conditioned
An animal with excess flesh and patchy fat deposits, especially over the shoulders, back, hips, and thighs.

Ovipositor
The organ with which an insect deposits its eggs.

Oxygen
A gas present in the air and necessary to breathing.

Pacemaker
A horse that takes the lead and sets the speed for a race.

Paddock
A grassy enclosure in which horses can be turned out. The enclosure at a racetrack in which horses are prepared for a race.

Parakeratosis
Mode of keratinization characterized by the retention of nuclei in the stratum corneum. In the skin, this process leads to the abnormal replacement of annular squams with nucleated cells.

Parenteral
Administration by injection, not through the digestive tract (e.g., subcutaneous, intramuscular, intrasternal, intravenous).

Parimutual
A form of betting in which the total amount wagered, after a percentage is deducted for costs, is divided among the holders of winning tickets.

Parity price
A level of farm prices intended to provide the same approximate purchasing power for farmers as enjoyed during a preceding base period.

Parrot mouth
A malformed mouth of an animal in which the upper jaw abnormally protrudes beyond the lower jaw.

Particle
A minute portion of matter.

Parts per billion (Ppb)
Equal to micrograms per kilogram or microliters per liter.

Parts per million (Ppm)
Equal to milligrams per kilogram or milliliters per liter.

Parturition
The act or process of giving birth to young.

Pass
Failure to conceive.

Passage
A dressage movement. Looks like an exaggerated trot.

Pasture
Plants, such as grass, grown for feeding or grazing animals. Also to feed cattle and other livestock on pasture.

Pathogen
Any microorganism that produces disease (bacteria, viruses, yeasts, molds, and parasites).

Peck
Eight gallons.

Pediculicide
A chemical that destroys lice.

Pedigree
A record of an animal's ancestors, usually only those of the five closest generations.

Pelt
Animal skin and fur.

Pendulous udders
Loosely attached udder.

Perennial
Living through several years. All trees are perennial.

Perfecta
See exacta.

Permanent identification
Identification that stays with the animal for its lifetime and cannot be lost. Examples are tattoos, color markings (sketch or photo), and hot or freeze brand. *See unique identification.*

Petal
A single leaf of the corolla.

pH
A logarithmic measure of the acidity or alkalinity of a solution using the hydrogen ion concentration. The pH scale ranges from 0 to 14 with numbers above 7 being alkaline and numbers below 7, acidic. A one number change means the solution is ten times weaker or stronger than the previous measure.

Phenotype
The expression of genes that can be measured by our senses--what we physically see of some trait in an animal.

Phosphate
An ion of phosphorus and oxygen (H_2PO_4- or HPO_4-2). May exist as an ion in solution or as an ester or salt of phosphoric acid.

Phosphoric acid
An important plant food occurring in bones and rock phosphates.

Pica
A craving for unnatural articles of food as observed in phosphorus-deficient animals. A depraved appetite.

Pink eye (conjunctivitis)

An inflammatory disease of the eye. The eye may become pearl colored and opaque leading to blindness.

Pipeline

A stainless steel or glass pipe used for transporting milk by gravity to storage. May be above the milking units (high line) or below the level of the units (low line).

Pistil

The part of the blossom that contains the immature seeds.

Placenta

The tissue attachment between the fetus and the mother.

Plain

A term suggesting general inferiority. Coarse. Lacking the desired quality or breed character.

Plasma

The liquid portion of blood or lymph in which corpuscles or blood cells float.

Poll

The top part of a horse's head located just between the ears.

Polled

Describes a hornless animal.

Pollen

The powdery substance born by the stamen of the flower. It is necessary for seed production.

Pollination

The act of carrying pollen from stamens to pistils. It is usually done by the wind or insects.

Polygastric
  Possessing more than one stomach compartment, as do cows and other ruminant animals.

Pony
  Any horse less than 14.2 hands (58 inches) when fully grown.

Porosity
  The state of having small openings or passages between the particles of matter.

Post
  Either the starting or finishing point at a racetrack. To rise up from the saddle while a horse is trotting.

Post-legged
  A condition in which the hind legs are too straight so that the springy quality of the hock and pastern is lost.

Postpartum
  Occurring after birth of the offspring.

Potash
  An oxide of potassium (K_2O) used as a plant nutrient or fertilizer.

Predicted transmitting ability (PTA)
  An estimation of an animal's potential to transmit yield productivity to its offspring based on pedigree information and the animal's performance, if available.

Prepartum
  Occurring before birth of the offspring.

Prepotent
  Designating an animal that transmits its own character to its progeny to a marked or highly uniform degree.

Prepping
  Preparing a horse for a sale, race, show, etc.

Primary waste treatment
   The initial treatment of waste water to reduce pollution potential or health hazard. With animal manure, an example would be *liquid-solid separation*.

Processing
   The process of killing and preparing an animal for market.

Produce
   Female's offspring.

Production and type index (PTI)
   Combines genetic merit measurements for production and type in a ratio thus ranking sires on their ability to transmit a balance of these traits.

Progeny testing
   Evaluating the genotype of an individual by a study of its offspring. An evaluation of the transmitting ability of an individual based on the performance of offspring.

Prolapsed uterus
   A condition in which the uterus is partially or completely turned inside out, outside the animal's body, usually following parturition.

Propagate
   To cause plants or animals to increase in number.

Protein
   The name of a group of substances containing nitrogen. It is one of the most important of feeding stuffs.

Protein equivalent
   A term indicating the total nitrogen content of a substance in comparison with the nitrogen content of protein, usually plant. For example, the non-protein nitrogen (NPN) compound, urea, contains approximately 45 percent nitrogen and has a protein equivalent of 281 percent (6.25 x 45 percent).

Protein supplements
Feed products that contain 20 percent or more of protein.

Proximate analysis
Tests for nitrogen (crude protein), crude fiber, ether extract (lipids), and ash which, with nitrogen-free extract, represent the gross composition of feed.

Pruning
Trimming or cutting parts that are not needed or that are injurious.

Pseudo-pregnancy
17 day period during which a female does not conceive. The female exhibits symptoms of hormonal balance simulating pregnancy.

Psychrophilic
Cold-loving. Refers to microorganisms that grow best at refrigerated temperatures, that is, 4° to 15°C.

Psychrotrophic
Cold-tolerant. Refers to microorganisms that grow at low temperatures, 4° to 15°C, but may have an optimum temperature above this range.

Pulverize
To reduce to a dust-like state.

Pupa
An insect in the stage of its life that comes just before the adult stage.

Purebred
The offspring of purebred parents of the same breed. Ancestors of purebreds can be traced to foundation stock in the original herd book. An animal with two registered parents of the same breed. Purebreds are not all registered.

Purity (of seed)

Seeds are pure when they contain only one kind of seed and no foreign matter.

Pus

A liquid product of inflammation consisting of leukocytes, lymph, bacteria, dead tissue cells, and fluid derived from their decomposition.

Pyometra

An accumulation of pus in the uterus.

Q fever

An acute infectious disease caused by Coxiella burnetti. It is characterized by a sudden onset of fever, headache, malaise, and weakness. In humans, it is commonly contracted by inhaling infected dusts derived from infected domestic animals.

Qualitative risk assessment

A risk assessment based on data which, although insufficient for numerical risk estimations, allows risk ranking or separation into descriptive categories of risk, and identification of inherent uncertainty.

Quality-adjusted life year (QALY)

A generic measure of disease burden, including both the quality and quantity of life lived. It is used in assessing the value of money for medical intervention.

Quantitative genetics

The area of genetics concerned with the inheritance of continuously-varying traits.

Quantitative polymerase chain reaction

Methods used for detecting the amplified DNA products from the polymerase chain reaction as they accumulate, instead of at the end of the reaction.

Quantitative risk assessment

A risk assessment that uses numerical expressions of risk and indication of inherent uncertainty.

Quarg

A soft, unripened, fresh cheese that is close to the consistency of yogurt.

Quarters

The hindquarters. The area of an animal's body extending from the rear of the flank to the root of the tail and downwards to the tops of the hind legs.

Quinella

A bet in which the first two places in a race must be predicted, but not necessarily in the correct order.

Rabbit
A domesticated rodent of the genus *Orctolagus Cuniculus*.

Rabbit dietary fiber
The types of fiber found to be most beneficial to the digestive system of rabbits.

Rabbitry
Place where domestic rabbits are kept. A rabbit-raising enterprise.

Racing plate
A thin, lightweight horseshoe used for racing.

Rails
Horizontal bars that make a jump.

Ranchers
People who raise livestock on rangeland.

Rate of passage
The time taken by undigested residues from a given meal to reach the feces.

Ration
The food allowed an animal for 24 hours. *See balanced ration*.

Ratites
Large flightless birds having small or rudimentary wings and breastbones lacking a keel. Ostriches and emus are ratites.

Recalcitrant

The portion of a nutrient in the soil that is unavailable for biochemical activity or plant uptake.

Recessive

Non-dominant gene. Only manifests when a gene of both parents is the same.

Red ribbon

A piece of red ribbon tied around a horse's tail to indicate that it is known to kick.

Refusal

The failure of a horse to try to jump an obstacle, either by stopping in front of it, or by going around it.

Registered

Purebred animal registered in the herdbook of the proper breed association. Certain associations (for example, the Red and White association) will register non- purebred animals providing they satisfy certain other criteria.

Registration

The process of certifying that an animal meets the qualifications established by the breed association for that breed and has a three-generation pedigree. Requires examination by a licensed registrar.

Registration certificate

Proof that the parentage of an animal is known and is recorded in the Breed Registry Herdbook.

Regression analysis

Procedures for finding the mathematical function which best describe the relationship between a dependent variable and one or more independent variables.

Regurgitate

To cast up undigested food from the stomach to the mouth, as done by ruminants.

Rein back
To make a horse step backward while being ridden.

Reins
Long, narrow, leather strips used to control the horse. One end is attached to the bit, the other end is held by the rider.

Resistance
The act of refusing to go forward, stop, run back, or rear.

Resistant
A plant is resistant to disease when it can ward off attacks of the disease.

Retained placenta
Placental membranes not expelled normally at parturition.

Retort pouches
A flexible package in which food is sterilized and hermetically sealed for long-term unrefrigerated storage.

Ride
To be transported in a mounted position.

Ringer
A horse entered in a race under the name of another, to win bets illegally by making one who bets and bookmakers believe they are betting on an inferior horse.

Rogue
Bad tempered horse.

Rotation of crops
A well-arranged succession of different crops on the same land.

Roughage

Consists of pasture, silage, hay, or other dry fodder. It may be of high or low quality. Roughages are usually high in crude fiber (more than 18 percent) and relatively low in NFE (approximately 40 percent).

Roundworm

Ascarids, an internal parasite.

Rugged

When referencing an animal, large and strong.

Rump

The hind portion of the back and bones.

Run on

To graze or pasture on, as for horses to run on the range.

Run out

To avoid an obstacle which is to be jumped by running around it or to pass on the wrong side of a marker flag.

Runoff

The portion of rainfall or irrigation water draining from fields into surface streams or bodies of water. May carry pollutants from field surfaces.

Saddle
The rounded, intermediate portion of the back between the shoulder and loin. The device a rider sits on.

Sanitize
To kill or remove injurious microorganisms but not necessarily to sterilize. Dairy equipment is commonly sanitized with heat or chemicals.

Scale
The overall size of an animal.

School
To train for a specific purpose. An area for training.

Scion
A shoot, sprout, or branch taken to graft or bud upon another plant.

Scours
A persistent diarrhea in animals.

Scratch
To withdraw from an event after officially entering. To spur a horse vigorously.

Scrub
An animal from non-purebred parents and doesn't show the predominant characteristics of any breed.

Secondary waste treatment
A second treatment of waste water to reduce pollution potential or health hazard.

Seed bed
The layer of earth in which seeds are sown.

Seed selection
The careful selection of seed from particular plants with the object of keeping or increasing a desirable quality.

Seedling
A young plant just from the seed.

Selection
The causing or allowing of certain individuals in a population to produce the next generation. Artificial selection is that practiced by man; natural selection is that practiced by nature.

Selection intensity
The margin of true genetic superiority of those animals selected in comparison to all those from which the choices were made.

Self-feeder
A feeding system that allows animals to eat at will.

Septicemia
The presence of microorganisms and their associated poisons in the blood (commonly called blood poisoning).

Serotype
The type of microorganism as determined by the kind and combination of constituent antigens associated with the cell.

Service
A term commonly used in animal breeding, denoting the mating of male to female. Also called serving or covering.

Service sire
   The sire to which a female is bred.

Settled
   Term used to indicate that an animal has become pregnant.

Settling basin
   Any area that reduces flow velocity and allows particulates to settle from a liquid suspension. Usually built to allow solids removal on a regular basis.

Shelf life
   The time after processing during which a product remains suitable for human consumption.

Shoes
   Metal plates that fit around the outer edges of the hooves to protect them from injury and wear.

Shy
   To move away suddenly because of a sound or obstacle.

Shy breeder
   A male or female of any domesticated livestock that has a low reproductive efficiency.

Sib (sibling)
   A brother or sister.

Sickle-hocked
   Describes an animal having a crooked hock, which causes the lower part of the leg to be bent forward out of a normal perpendicular straight line.

Silage
   Green forage, such as grass, clover, fodder, field corn, or sorghum, that is chopped into a silo, where it is packed or compressed to exclude air and undergoes an acid fermentation (lactic and acetic acids) that slows spoilage.

Silks

The cap and blouse worn by a racing jockey which carry the owner's colors.

Silo

A vertical cylindrical structure, pit, trench, or other relatively airtight chamber in which chopped green crops, such as corn, grass, legumes, or small grain and other livestock feeds are fermented and stored.

Sire

The male parent. To father or beget.

Sire selection

Process of identifying males to be used as service sires with the goal of increasing the genetic potential of the herd.

Sketch (photo)

A method of permanent identification to be cross-referenced with visible identification.

Slip

To abort.

Slipping Coat

A coat that is shedding or molting a profusion of hairs.

Smut

A disease of plants, particularly of cereals, which causes all or part of the plant to become a powdery mass.

Snaffle bit

The oldest type of bit, consisting of a straight or jointed bit with a ring at each end to which the reins are attached.

Sock

White marking on any or all of an animal's lower leg.

Soilage
 Freshly cut green forage often fed to animals in drylot. Also called green chop.

Solvent-extracted
 Fat or oil removed from materials (such as soybean seeds) by organic solvents.

Sound
 Free from any illness, disease, blemish, imperfection, or defect which make an animal unable to function properly.

Spayed
 To have surgically removed the ovaries of a female animal.

Sphincter
 A ring-shaped muscle that closes an opening, such as the sphincter muscles in the lower end of a cow's teat.

Spike
 A lengthened flower cluster with stalkless flowers.

Spiracle
 An air opening in the body of an insect.

Spore
 A small body formed by a fungus to reproduce. It serves the same use as seeds for flowering plants.

Spray
 To apply a liquid in the form of a very fine mist by the aid of a pump for the purpose of killing fungi or insects.

Sprinter
 A horse which is able to cover short distances at great speed. Sprinters are rarely able to maintain a fast pace over long distances.

Stable

Building where animals are kept.

Stallion

An ungelded male horse more than four years old.

Stamen

The part of the flower that bears the pollen.

Stamina

Endurance.

Stanchion

A specially designed headgate to hold an animal in place while allowing feeding and resting.

Statistically significant

The likelihood that a result or relationship is caused by something other than mere random chance. Statistical Hypothesis Testing is traditionally employed to determine if a result is statistically significant.

Stayer

A horse which is able to cover long distances because of its strength, stamina, and endurance power.

Sterile

Unable to produce offspring.

Sterilize

To remove or kill all living organisms. To make barren or unproductive, such as a vasectomy in stallions.

Steward

An official who sees that rules are obeyed at a race or show.

Stigma

The part of the pistil that receives the pollen.

Stillborn

Born lifeless. Dead at birth.

Stover

Fodder. Mature cured stalks of grain from which seeds have been removed, such as stalks of corn without ears.

Strain

A race or stock of rabbits in any standard breed of the same family blood. Having the quality of reproducing marked radical characteristics.

Strangles

An infectious disease which is common among young horses. Symptoms include a high temperature, a thick nasal discharge, and swelling of the lymph glands.

Streak canal

See teat meatus.

String

A group of animals within a larger group or herd.

Strongyles

Highly contagious disease caused by parasites in the gastrointestinal tract of mammals. Especially in grazers such as sheep, cattle, and horses.

Stud

A place where breeding horses are kept. A stallion.

Subclinical

A disease condition without clinical manifestations.

Subcutaneous
Situated or occurring beneath the skin.

Succulence
A condition of plants characterized by juiciness, freshness, and tenderness, making them appetizing to animals.

Suckling
A foal which is nursing.

Sulphur
A yellowish chemical element. Brimstone.

Supplement
To add minerals, vitamins, or other minor ingredients to a ration.

Surcingle
A webbing belt used to keep the saddle in position which passes over the saddle and girth.

Swayback
An abnormally hollowed back, especially in horses. It can be caused by a deficiency of metabolizable copper in the mother during the last half of her pregnancy.

Sweetbreads
The thymus glands of veal, young beef, lamb, and pork used as food.

Sweetcorn
A variety of corn (Zea mays) with high sugar content and low starch content, eaten as a vegetable.

Swine erysipelas

An acute and chronic contagious disease of young pigs caused by a bacterium, Erysipelothrix Rhusiopathiae, characterized by inflammation and redness of the skin and subcutaneous tissues.

Swine vesicular disease

An enterovirus infection of swine that causes mild fever and blisters around the mouth and feet. Clinically indistinguishable from foot-and-mouth disease, vesicular stomatitis, and vesicular exanthema.

Tack
Riding gear, such as the saddle and bridle.

Take
To accept a male in coitus. Lay term meaning to become pregnant.

Tapeworm
Parasitic flatworm that lives in the intestines causing abdominal pain, diarrhea, and weight loss.

Taproot
The main root of a plant which runs directly down into the earth to a considerable depth without dividing.

Tattoo
Permanent ink used as a method of permanent identification to be cross- referenced with visible identification.

Teat
A small protuberance or appendage on the udder through which milk flows.

Teat meatus
Small canal located in the end of each teat. Also called a *streak canal*.

Temperature
The degree or intensity of heat present in a substance or object as shown by a thermometer.

Term
The gestation period.

Terrace
A ridge of earth run on a level around a slope or hillside to keep the land from washing away.

Tertiary waste treatment
The final treatment of waste water to reduce pollution potential or health hazard allowing discharge into bodies of water. Not economically practical with animal manure waste waters.

Tetanus
Bacterial infection which causes painful muscle spasms, particularly in the jaw and neck. It can also interfere with the ability to breathe.

Tetany
A condition in an animal in which there are localized, spasmodic muscular contractions.

Tether
To tie an animal with a rope or chain to allow grazing but prevent straying.

Texture
The character of fur as determined by feel or touch, such as fine or coarse texture.

Thermometer
An instrument for measuring heat.

Thorax
The middle part of the body of an insect. The thorax lies between the abdomen and the head.

Thrush (foot rot)
Inflammation of the frog of a horse's hoof, characterized by a foul-smelling discharge.

Tillage
> The act of preparing land for seed and keeping the ground in a proper state for the growth of crops.

Titer
> The quantity of a substance required to produce a reaction with a given volume of another substance, or the amount of one substance required to correspond with a given amount of another substance. Agglutination titer is the highest dilution of a serum that causes clumping of bacteria.

Toe out
> To walk with the feet pointed outward. Also called splay-footed.

Total digestible nutrients (TDN)
> A standard evaluation of the nutritional merit of a particular feed for farm animals which includes all the digestible organic nutrients such as protein, fiber, nitrogen-free extract, and lipids.

Total mixed ration (TMR)
> *See complete ration.*

Toxins
> The poisons produced by certain microorganisms. They are products of cell metabolism. The symptoms of bacterial diseases, such as diphtheria, tetanus, botulism, and staphylococcal food poisoning, are caused by toxins.

Toxoid
> A denatured toxin. It retains the ability to stimulate the formation of antitoxin in the body.

Trade barriers
> Rules and regulations that hamper the trade of commodities. Tariffs, fees for imported goods, and import limits or quotas are barriers to trade.

Transplant
> A plant grown in a bed with a view to being removed to other soil.

Trap
Two wheeled vehicle.

Tree
Frame of a saddle.

Trifecta
A type of bet in which the person placing the bet must choose the first, second, and third place winners and the order in which they finish in order to win.

Tubercle
A small, wart-like growth on the roots of legumes.

Turf
A course over which a horse race is held.

Turn on the forehand
A movement in which the horse pivots on the forelegs while performing concentric circles with the hind legs.

Turn on the quarters
A movement in which the horse pivots on the hind legs while performing concentric circles with the forelegs.

Twitch
Tool used to restrain a horse.

Type
The physical conformation of an animal.

Type classification
A program sponsored by breed associations whereby a registered animal's conformation may be compared with the "ideal" or "true" type animal of that breed by an official inspector (classifier).

Typical
A term describing an ideal representative of any given breed or variety as applied to type, color, or fur quality.

Udder
The encased group of mammary glands provided with teats or nipples, as in a cow, ewe, mare, or sow. Also called a bag.

Undegraded intake protein (UIP)
The portion of intake protein escaping breakdown by rumen microorganisms.

Ungulate
A hoofed four-legged animal.

Unique identification
A series of non-duplicating numbers such as registration, uniform series ear tag, or VIP number. These numbers are cross-referenced with permanent identification for registered, VIP, and other recorded nonregistered animals. *See visible identification.*

United States Department of Agriculture (USDA)
The branch of the Federal government that is administered by the Secretary of Agriculture appointed by the President of the United States.

United States Pharmacopeia (USP)
A unit of measurement or potency of biologicals that usually coincides with an international unit. *See International Unit.*

Unsaturated fat
A fat having one or more double bonds, not completely hydrogenated.

Unshod

Horse not wearing shoes.

Unsound

An animal with a defect which makes it unable to function properly.

Unthriftiness

Lack of vigor, poor growth, or development. The quality or state of being unthrifty in animals.

Urea

A nonprotein organic nitrogenous compound (NH_2CONH_2). It is made synthetically by combining ammonia and carbon dioxide.

Uterus

Organ in the female in which developing fetuses are contained and nourished before birth.

Vaccination
The process of artificially stimulating the immune response to an altered biological material resulting in resistance to an infectious disease.

Variety
The quality or state of being different or diverse. The absence of uniformity, sameness, or monotony.

Ventilate
To open to the free passage of air.

Vice
Bad or immoral behavior or habits.

Virgin soil
Soil which has never been cultivated.

Virulence
The degree of pathogenicity (ability of produce disease) of a microorganism as indicated by case fatality rates and/or its ability to invade the tissues of a host.

Viscera
The internal organs of the body.

Visible identification
A readily visible numbering system attached to the animal that is used to easily identify the animal.

Vitality

The ability to grow.

Vitamins

Complex organic substances found in plant and animal tissue; necessary for control of metabolic processes. *See metabolize.*

Volatile fatty acids (VFA)

Commonly used in reference to acetic, propionic, and butyric acids produced in the rumen of cattle, goats, and sheep, in the cecum of sheep, the cecum and colon of swine, the colon of the horse, and the cecum of the rabbit.

Volatilization

The loss of gaseous materials, such as ammonia nitrogen, from animal manures to the atmosphere.

Wagon
Four-wheeled vehicle.

Warm-blood
A horse whose ancestors include both cold-bloods and hot-bloods.

Warrens
Outside pens where groups, or colonies, of rabbits are raised.

Weaner
Newly weaned animal.

Weaning
Denying young animals its mother's milk and switching it to solid foods.

Weathering
The action of moisture, air, and frost upon objects.

Weed
Any plant growing in a place in which it is not wanted.

Well turned-out
A horse/rider team which is well-groomed and well-dressed in competitions in which appearance is considered in judging.

Whinny
A gentle high-pitched neigh.

Win
To finish in first place.

Windgall
The puffy swelling of a horse's knee or fetlock joints, caused by an over secretion of the fluid in the joints.

Windsucking
A harmful habit in which a horse sucks in and swallows air, causing indigestion.

Wing shoulder
A condition in which the shoulder joint is away from the rib structure and skeleton (much of the skin is tucked in behind it).

Withers
Highest part of a horse's back, lying at the base of the neck above the shoulders. The height of a horse is measured to the withers.

Wolf teeth
Protruding or elongated teeth in the upper and lower jaw caused by improper alignment of the upper and lower front teeth preventing normal eating.

Womb
See uterus.

Wood wool
Fine wood shavings used in surgical dressings, bindings for plaster, nesting materials for animals, and insulating and packing materials.

Wry tail
Tail-head set either to the right or left of center.

Xanthan gum
A substance produced by bacterial fermentation or synthetically, and is used in foods as a gelling agent and thickener.

Xenophon
Father of classical horsemanship.

Xerophytes
A plant that needs very little water to survive, such as a cactus.

Xylem
A vascular plant tissue that conducts water and dissolved nutrients upwards from the roots to the leaves. Also helps to form the woody element in the stem.

Yearling
A horse between one and two years old. All foals born in a given year turn yearlings on the 1st of January (the universal birth date) following the date they were foaled.

Yeasts
A microscopic fungus consisting of single oval cells that reproduce by budding and are capable of converting sugar into alcohol and carbon dioxide.

Yield components
Plant parts contributing to yield based on their number, size, and weight.

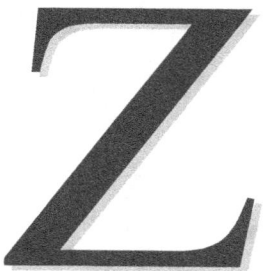

Zero emissions

Pollution abatement objective in which industrial processes and energy source emissions contribute no waste products such as greenhouse gases that pollute the environment or effect climate change.

Zero wastes

Waste management objective in which industrial outputs are reused as inputs and products are recycled to eliminate waste.

Zoonosis

Any disease which can be transmitted from animals to humans.

Zooplankton

Free-floating, often microscopic animals of aquatic systems. They include protozoa, rotifers, crustaceans, and larvae of larger animals that feed on other plankton.

Zygospores

The thick-walled resting cell of certain fungi and algae, arising from the fusion of two similar gametes.

www.ingramcontent.com/pod-product-compliance
Lightning Source LLC
Chambersburg PA
CBHW062046280526
45788CB00003B/1127